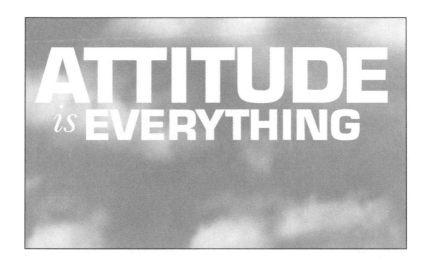

ATTITUDE is EVERYTHING

compiled by
Peggy M. Anderson

SUCCESSORIES LIBRARY

ATTITUDE IS EVERYTHING ©2000
Published by Career Press, Inc. All rights
reserved. Printed in the USA. No part of this book
may be reproduced or used in any form whatsoever
without prior written permission of the publisher.
For information, write Career Press, Inc., 3 Tice Road, Franklin
Lakes, NJ 07417

Library of Congress CIP information available on request.

Book Design: Michael McKee, Kevin McHugh

ISBN: 1-56414-39-9

Dedicated with love to my son Blayke.

Peggy M. Anderson

"If you never accept a challenge, you will never feel the excitement of victory."

"Refusing to accept anything but the best means you will probably get it."

"If it is to be, it is up to me."

"There are two things to aim at in life: to get what you want and, after that, to positively enjoy it."
Logan Pearsall

"The happiest people seem to be those who have no particular cause for being happy, except that they are so."

William Ralph Inge

3

*"To love what you do and feel that it matters —
how could anything be more fun?"*
Katherine Graham

"There is always room at the top."
Daniel Webster

*"Always do one thing more
than you think you can."*

*"If you think you can, you can.
And if you think you can't, you're right."*
Mary Kay Ash

"When you reach for the stars, you may not quite get one, but you won't come up with a handful of mud either."

"The way to overcome shyness is to become so wrapped up in something that you forget to be afraid."

Lady Bird Johnson

"We all have possibilities
we don't know about.
We can do things we
don't even dream
we can do."

Dale Carnegie

*"Big shots are only
little shots who keep shooting."*
Christopher Morley

*"Reflect on your present blessings, of which
every man has many; not on your past
misfortunes, of which all men have some."*
Charles Dickens

*"Do not wait for extraordinary situations
to do good; try to use ordinary situations."*
Jean Paul Richter

*"If you aspire to the highest place,
it is no disgrace to stop at the second,
or even the third place."*
Cicero

"Bite off more than you can chew, then chew it. Plan more than you can do, then do it."

"It is better to follow even the shadow of the best, than to remain content with the worst."

Henry Van Dyke

"You are too great for small dreams."

"To live happily is an inward
power of the soul."
Marcus Aurelius

---

*"A sailor without a destination
cannot hope for a favorable wind."*
Leon Tec, M.D.

*"Seize from every moment its unique novelty
and do not prepare your joys."*
André Gide

*"Keep your face to the sun,
and you will never see
the shadows."*

Helen Keller

13

*"Make your life a mission —
not an intermission."*
Arnold Glasgow

*"Hit the ball over the fence and you can
take your time going around the bases."*
John W. Roper

*"Do better work than any other man
in your field — and keep on doing it."*
Wilfred A. Peterson

"Grow like a tree, not like a mushroom."
Janet Erskine Stuart

"Ascend above the restrictions and conventions of the world, but not so high as to lose sight of them."

Richard Garnett

"In great attempts, it is glorious even to fail."

Vincent Lombardi

"Nothing great was ever achieved without great men, and men are great only if they are determined to be so."

Charles DeGaulle

"You can always pitch better."
Sandy Koufax

"Think things through —
then follow through."
Edward Vernon Rickenbacker

"First say to yourself what you would be;
and then do what you have to do."
Epictetus

"You may be disappointed if you fail,
but you are doomed if you don't try."
Beverly Sills

"The future belongs to those who believe in the beauty of their dreams."

"Aim at the sun, and you may not reach it; but your arrow will fly higher than if aimed at an object on a level with yourself."

Joel Hawes

"Love your life."
Henry David Thoreau

*"When fate hands us a lemon,
let's try to make lemonade."*
Dale Carnegie

*"Never lose an opportunity to see
the beauty within God's creation."*

*"It is hard to fail, but it is worse
never to have tried to succeed."*

Theodore Roosevelt

"Keep on going and the chances are you will stumble on something, perhaps when you are least expecting it. I have never heard of anyone stumbling on something sitting down."

Charles F. Kettering

23

"Our mind determines our attitude."

*"You cannot always control circumstances.
But you can control your own thoughts."*
Charles E. Popplestone

"Any fact facing us is not as important as our attitude toward it, for that determines our success or failure."

Norman Vincent Peale

"When you get to the end of your rope, tie a knot and hang on."

Franklin D. Roosevelt

> *"Become all that you
> are capable of becoming."*
> *Robert J. McKain*

> *"Positive thinking is reacting
> positively to a negative situation."*
> *Bill Havens*

"If you doubt you can accomplish something, then you can't accomplish it. You have to have confidence in your ability, and then be tough enough to follow through."

Rosalynn Carter

*"It is the way we react to circumstances
that determines our feeling."*
Dale Carnegie

*"If you occasionally fall — and we all do —
just be sure to fall forward."*

*"The only lack or limitation is
in your own mind."*

N.H. Moos

*"I will prepare and someday
my chance will come."*

Abraham Lincoln

*"You are the only one who
can stretch your own horizon."*
Edgar F. Magnin

*"You will become as small as your
controlling desire; or as great as your
dominant aspiration."*
James Allen

> *"Man's greatness lies in his power of thought."*
>
> *Blaise Pascal*

> *"A man can succeed at almost anything for which he has unlimited enthusiasm."*
>
> *Charles Schwab*

"Don't curse the darkness — light a candle."
Chinese Proverb

*"Think little goals and expect little
achievements. Think big goals
and win big success."*
David Joseph Schwartz

"Make no little plans; they have no magic to stir men's blood... Make big plans, aim high in hope, and work."

Daniel H. Burnham

"It is not the situation...
It's your reaction to the situation."
Bob Conklin

"You have to expect things of yourself
before you can do them."
Michael Jordan

"Pessimism never won any battles."

Dwight D. Eisenhower

*"The measure of a man is the way
he bears up under misfortune."*

Plutarch

*"We are what we think.
All that we are arises with our thoughts.
With our thoughts, we make our world."*
Buddha

*"Nothing external to you
has any power over you."*
Ralph Waldo Emerson

"Reach high, for stars lie hidden in your soul. Dream deep, for every dream precedes the goal."

Pamela Starr

*"We don't get what we want.
We get what we are."*

*"Thy actions, and thy actions alone,
determine thy worth."*

Johann Fichte

*For every obstacle there is a solution —
over, under, around, and through."*

*"You are successful the moment you start
moving toward a worthwhile goal."*
Chuck Carlson

*"Winners expect to win in advance.
Life is a self-fulfilling prophecy."*

"Light tomorrow with today!"
Elizabeth Barrett Browning

"You cannot take charge of the present if you are busy reliving the setbacks of the past."

Newman & Berkowitz

"He who reins within himself and rules passions, desires, and fears is more than a king."

John Milton

"A clear understanding of negative emotions dismisses them."

Vernon Howard

"The roots of true achievement lie in the will to become the best that you can become."

Harold Taylor

*"If you can't do great things,
do small things in a great way.
Don't wait for great opportunities.
Seize common, everyday ones and
make them great."*

Napoleon Hill

"The best way to secure future happiness is to be as happy as is rightfully possible today."

Charles W. Eliot

"Nothing can stop the man with the right mental attitude from achieving his goal; nothing on earth can help the man with the wrong mental attitude."

Thomas Jefferson

*"When we direct our thoughts,
we can control our emotions."*

W. Clement Stone

*"Your range of available choices,
right now, is limitless."*

Carl Frederick

"To change your attitude is to change your life."

"Life is either a daring adventure or nothing."

Helen Keller

"I see that my steadfast desire was alone responsible for whatever progress or mastery I have made. The reality is always there, and is preceded by vision. And if one keeps looking steadily the vision crystallizes into fact or deed."

Henry Miller

47

"Life is what your thoughts make it."
Marcus Aurelius

*"A positive attitude is not a destination.
It is a way of life."*

*"It is never too late to be
what you might have become."*

George Eliot

*"The foolish person seeks happiness in the
distance, the wise grow it under their feet."*

James Oppenheim

"Success is an inside job."
Ralph M. Ford

*"It is often the last key on the
ring that opens the door."*

*"Your mind will give back exactly
what you put into it."*

"The ripest peach is the highest on the tree."
James Whitcomb

"No one knows what he can do till he tries."
Publilius Syrus

"The one thing that matters is the effect."
Antoine De Saint-Exupéry

"I would sooner fail, than not be among the greatest."

John Keats

53

*"Not in time, place, or circumstances,
but in the man lies success."*

Charles B. Rouss

"No one will do it for you."

Ben Stein

"Everything is possible for him who believes."
Bible, Mark 9:23

*"To win without risk is to
triumph without glory."*
Pierre Corneille

*"Give me beauty in the inward soul
and the outward man will be at one."*

*"If we do what is necessary,
all the odds are in our favor."*

Henry Kissinger

*"All that a man achieves
and all that he fails to achieve
is the direct result of his
own thoughts."*

James Allen

> *"Do a little more each day than*
> *you think you possibly can."*
>
> *Lowell Thomas*

> *"There's a way to do it better — find it."*
>
> *Thomas A. Edison*

*"When you expect things to happen,
strangely enough, they do."*
John J. B. Morgan

"Fall seven times, stand up eight."
Japanese Proverb

*"The doors we open and close each day,
decide the lives we live."*

Flora Whittemore

"Hitch your wagon to a star."

Ralph Waldo Emerson

"Much effort, much prosperity."
Euripides

*"The joyfulness of a man
prolongeth his days."*

"Man is not made for defeat."
Ernest Hemingway

"People need joy as much as clothing."
Margaret Collier Graham

"What happens is not as important as how you react to what happens."

J. G. Gallimore

"Happiness is a habit — cultivate it."
Elbert Hubbard

*"Sooner or later, those who win
are those who think they can."*
Richard Bach

"You win only if you aren't afraid to lose."
Rocky Aoki

"No man fails who does his best."
Orison Swett Marden

"Joy comes from using your potential."
Will Schultz

*"Happiness is not in having
or being; it is in doing."*
Lilian Eichler Watson

*"One person can make a
difference and every
person should try."*

John F. Kennedy

"We will not know unless we begin."
Howard Zinn

"If you get up the courage to begin,
you have the courage to succeed."
David Viscott

*"The man who believes he can do something
is probably right, and so is the man
who believes he can't."*

*"Don't wait for your ship to come in,
swim out to it."*

*"No problem can stand the
assault of sustained thinking."*
Voltaire

*"Accept the challenges, so that you may
feel the exhilaration of victory."*
General George S. Patton

"When you bombard yourself with inward success, you don't have time to be negative."

Frank Meyer

"If you are all wrapped up in yourself, you are overdressed."

Kate Halverson

*"Go for the moon. If you don't get it,
you'll still be heading for a star."*

*"Happiness lies not in the mere possession of
money; it lies in the joy of achievement,
in the thrill of creative effort."*

Franklin D. Roosevelt

"You don't get to choose how you're going to die, or when. You can only decide how you're going to live."

Joan Baez

*"The soul can split the sky in two
and let the face of God shine through."*
Edna St. Vincent Millay

"Winning starts with beginning."
Robert H. Schuller

"It is impossible to win the race unless you venture to run, impossible to win a victory unless you dare to battle."

Richard M. De Vos

"All times are beautiful for those who manage joy within them."

Rosalina de Castro

"For every failure, there's an alternative course of action. You just have to find it. When you come to a roadblock, take a detour."

Mary Kay Ash

"A misty morning does not signify a cloudy day."

"Act well at the moment, and you have performed a good action for all eternity."

Johann K. Lavater

"The happiness of your life depends upon the character of your thoughts."

"They conquer who believe they can."
John Dryden

"Choice, not chance, determines destiny."

*"You cannot control the length of your life,
but you can control its breadth,
depth, and height."*

"Hope is a waking dream."

*"Every man is the architect
of his own fortune."*
Appius Claudius

"You've got to believe deep inside yourself
that you're destined to do great things."
Joe Paterno

"We must always change, renew, rejuvenate
ourselves; otherwise we harden."
Goethe

*"Slumber not in the tents of your fathers.
The world is advancing — advance with it."*

Giuseppe Mazzini

*"Attempt the impossible in order
to improve your work."*

Bette Davis

*"Cultivate your garden.
Do not depend upon teachers
to educate you...follow your
own bent, pursue your curiosity
bravely, express yourself, make
your own harmony."*

Will Durant

> *"Don't be afraid to give up
> the good, to go for the great."*
> *Kenny Rogers*

> *"First say to yourself what you would be;
> and then do what you have to do."*
> *Epictetus*

*"Be absolutely determined
to enjoy what you do."*
Gerry Sikorski

*"As long as you're going to be
thinking anyway, think big."*
Donald Trump

"You're never a loser until you quit trying."
Mike Ditka

"See the invisible, feel the intangible,
and achieve the impossible."

*"Take each good day
and relish each moment.
Take each bad day and
work to make it good."*

Lisa Dado

---

*"Take care to get what you like or you
will be forced to like what you do."*
George Bernard Shaw

*"In the long run men hit only
what they aim at."*
Henry David Thoreau

*"The final forming of a person's
character lies in their own hands."*

Anne Frank

"Adventure is worthwhile in itself."

Amelia Earhart

*"Be grateful for what you have,
not regretful for what you haven't."*

*"Thoughts are energy, and you can make your
world or break your world by your thinking."*
Susan L. Taylor

*"Keep your heart free from hate, your mind
from worry...expect little, give much."*

*"The ultimate goal should be
doing your best and enjoying it."*
Peggy Fleming

"Some succeed because they are destined to, but most succeed because they are determined to."

"Use what talents you possess. The woods would be very silent if no birds sang there except those that sang best."

Henry Van Dyke

> *"Ride on! Rough-shod if need be, smooth-shod if that will do, but ride on! Ride on over all obstacles, and win the race."*

Charles Dickens

93

"Pursue worthy aims."
Solon

*"Do your job brilliantly and
the cream will rise to the top."*
Irene Rosenfeld

*"Toil to make yourself remarkable
by some talent or other."*
Seneca

*"The secret of success is
constancy to purpose."*
Benjamin Disraeli

"Put yourself on view.
This brings your talents to light."
Baltasar Gracian

"Have a purpose in life, and having it throw
into your work such strength of mind
and muscle as God has given you."
Thomas Carlyle

"Have fun doing whatever it is that you desire to accomplish... and do it because you love it, not because it's work."

Paul Westphal

"Believe in yourself!
Have faith in your abilities.
Remind yourself that God is with
you and nothing can defeat you."
Norman Vincent Peale

"They can do all because they think they can."
Virgil

> *"A wise man will make more
> opportunities than he finds."*
>
> *Francis Bacon*

> *"If there is no wind, row."*
>
> *Latin Proverb*

"Do what you can, where you are, with what you've got."

Theodore Roosevelt

"Nothing is impossible; there are ways that lead to everything."

Francois de la Rochefoucauld

*"Most of us can do more than we think we can,
but usually do less than we think we do."*

*"Resolve to be thyself; and know that he
who finds himself loses his misery."*
Matthew Arnold

*"You can't steal second base
and keep one foot on first."*

*"Your living is determined not so
much by what life brings to you as
by the attitude you bring to life."*

John Homer Miller

"If you have built castles in the air, your work need not be lost; that is where they should be. Now put the foundations under them."

Henry David Thoreau

> *"One of the rarest things that man
> does is to do the best he can."*
>
> *Josh Billings*

> *"You have got to make it happen."*
>
> *Joe Greene*

"If you can't think up a new idea, try finding a way to make better use of an old idea."

"No one can cheat you out of ultimate success but yourself."

Ralph Waldo Emerson

"You have to expect things of yourself before you can do them."
Michael Jordon

"The journey of a thousand miles, starts with a single step."
Chinese Proverb

> *"Our greatest weakness lies in giving up. The most certain way to succeed is to always try just one more time."*

Thomas Edison

*"You can't climb uphill
by thinking downhill thoughts."*

*"When you're through changing,
you're through."*

Bruce Barton

> *"Things don't turn up in this world*
> *until somebody turns them up."*
> James Garfield

> *"Help yourself, and Heaven will help you."*
> La Fontaine

*"Be not afraid of growing slowly,
be afraid of standing still."*
Chinese Proverb

"Lift where you stand."
Edward Everett Hale

"Joy is not in things, it is in us."
Richard Wagner

"Don't complain because you don't have…
Enjoy what you've got."
H. Stanley Judd

*"To accomplish great things,
we must dream as well as act."*

Anatole France

"Determine never to be idle."

Thomas Jefferson

"The greatest mistake a man can make, is to be afraid of making one."

Elbert Hubbard

*"Why not go out on a limb?
Isn't that where the fruit is?"*
Frank Scully

"Begin at once to live."
Seneca

*"He who does not hope to win
has already lost."*

Jose Juaquin Olmedo

"Nothing is impossible to a willing heart."

John Heywood

"If you do not believe in yourself, few other people will."

"One can walk over the highest mountain one step at a time."

John Wanamaker

"Everything starts with yourself — with you making up your mind about what you're going to do with your life."

Tony Dorsett

117

"Doubt whom you will, but never yourself."
Christine Bowee

*"Do not despise the bottom rungs
in the ascent to greatness."*
Publilius Syrus

"If you want to be respected,
you must respect yourself."

Spanish Proverb

"If you don't run your own life,
somebody else will."

John Atkinson

*"Everything depends upon
the way we look at things."*

Orison Swett Marden

*"Every great achievement
is the story of a flaming heart."*

Harry Truman

*"You must do the thing
you think you cannot do."*
Eleanor Roosevelt

"The odds are with us if we keep on trying."
Keith De Green

> *"There is no future in any job.*
> *The future lies in the man who holds the job."*
>
> George W. Crane

> *"Make the iron hot by striking it."*
>
> Oliver Cromwell

"The golden opportunity you are seeking is in yourself. It is not in your environment; it is not in luck or chance, or the help of others; it is in yourself alone."

Orison Swett Marden

*"As long as you believe
in yourself, others will."*
Cynda Williams

*"Don't search for opportunities in a distance
until you have exhausted the advantages
of those right where you are."*
Jerry L. Jones Sr.

"It's never too late — never too late to start over, never too late to be happy."

Jane Fonda

"Your big opportunity may be right where you are now."

Napoleon Hill

"Try your ideals by visualizing them in action."

David Seabury

"You can't turn back the clock. But you can wind it up again."

Bonnie Prudden

"Mistakes are lessons in wisdom. The past cannot be changed. The future is yet in your power."

Hugh White

*"This one step — choosing a goal and
sticking to it — changes everything."*
Scott Reed

"You can plant a dream."
Anne Campbell

*"Dwell not upon your weariness,
your strength shall be according to
the measure of your desire."*

Arab Proverb

*"Fear not that thy life shall come to an end,
but rather fear that it shall never
have a beginning."*

John Henry Cardinal Newman

*"Never stand begging for that which
you have the power to earn."*

Miguel de Cervantes

*"Dream no small dreams, for they have
no power to move the hearts of men."*

Goethe

*"Too low they build,
who build beneath the stars."*

Edward Young

*"Cherish all your happy moments;
they make a fine cushion for old age."*

Christopher Morley

*"You must begin to think of yourself
as becoming the person you want to be."*
David Viscott

"Life gives nothing to a man without labor."
Horace

"Don't be afraid to give your best to what seemingly are small jobs. Every time you conquer one it makes you that much stronger. If you do little jobs well, the big ones will tend to take care of themselves."

Dale Carnegie

133

"The finest steel has to go through the hottest fire."

Richard M. Nixon

"Your own excellence, success, and greatest pride comes from only one person, you."

Frank Robinson

"We must open the doors of opportunity."
Lyndon B. Johnson

*"Life is a great big canvas, and you should
throw all the paint on it you can."*
Danny Kaye

---

*"One has to remember that every failure can
be a stepping-stone to something better."*
Colonel Harland Sanders

"Depend not on fortune, but on conduct."
Publilius Syrus

*"It is a funny thing about life,
if you refuse to accept
anything but the best,
you very often get it."*

Somerset Maugham

"Sit, walk, or run — but don't wobble."

"You must set the standard."
Charles H. Kellstadt

*"You must be resolutely determined
that whatever you do shall
always be the best of which
you are capable."*

Charles E. Popplestone

"What is possible is our highest duty."

William E. McLaren

"It is not the position but the disposition."
J. E. Dinger

"Destiny is not a matter of chance,
it's a matter of choice."

*"Our life is a reflection
of our attitudes."*

*"The only limit to our realization of tomorrow
will be our doubts of today."*

Franklin D. Roosevelt

"Your attitude determines your altitude."

*"Obstacles are what you will see
when you take your eyes off your goal."*

"Every year I live, I am more
convinced that the waste of
life lies in the love we have
not given and the powers
we have not used."

Mary Cholmondeley

143

*"I'm not going to get it close.
I'm going to make it."*
Tom Watson

*"Focus on the doughnut,
not on the hole."*

"A good beginning makes a good ending."
English Proverb

"The way to do things is to begin."
Horace Greeley

*"Knowing where you're going
is all you need to get there."*
Carl Frederick

*"We are not interested in
the possibilities of defeat."*
Queen Victoria

*"There is no failure
except in no longer trying.
There is no defeat
except from within."*

"Great works are performed not by strength, but by perseverance."

Samuel Johnson

"In the game of life, nothing is less important than the score at half time."

"If you start to take Vienna — take Vienna!"
Napoleon Bonaparte

"One can go a long way after one is tired."
French Proverb

"Defeat never comes to any man
until he admits it."

Josephus Daniels

"Those that see nothing but faults...
seek for nothing else."

Thomas Fuller

"Man is what he believes."

Anton Chekhov

*"How many opportunities present themselves
without us noticing them?"*